Beq

JOHN CABOT AND NEWFOUNDLAND

ALAN F. WILLIAMS

NEWFOUNDLAND HISTORICAL SOCIETY

1996

ISBN: 0-9680803-0-8

The Newfoundland Historical Society gratefully acknowledges the financial support of
the Johnson Family Foundation, through whose generosity a copy of this book will be presented to every 1997 high school graduate
in Newfoundland and Labrador; The John Cabot (1997) 500th Anniversary Corporation;
and the Government of Canada through the Canadian Studies Program, Department of Canadian Heritage.

Project Coordinator: Eleanor Dawson
Editor: James Hiller
Design: Beth Oberholtzer
Photography: Ned Pratt
Cartography (pp. 4, 26): Charles Conway
Cover: 'John Cabot Leaving Bristol',
painted by Harold Goodridge for the Newfoundland Historical Society in 1947.
Reproduced by permission of the artist's executors, and by courtesy of the Government of Newfoundland and Labrador.

Professor Alan Williams, a former head of the Geography Department at Memorial University,
now teaches in the Department of American and Canadian Studies at the University of Birmingham, England.

62,474

ver a century ago, all that popular historians could say about the discovery of Newfoundland by Europeans was that perhaps the Norse got there first, about 1000 CE, followed (more certainly) by the Cabots nearly 500 years later. Philip Tocque's account was typical, and provides an early example of Newfoundlanders' conviction that John Cabot's landfall was Cape Bonavista:

Some writers have affirmed that Newfoundland was discovered by the Scandinavians in the year 1001, while others assert that this alleged discovery by the Northmen is not worthy of credence... We, therefore, pass over the mists of romance and fable for the facts of history. The discovery of the West Indies by Columbus in 1492; and of Newfoundland by the Cabots, in 1497, is detailed in almost every book written on America...we shall proceed at once to say that John Cabot (or Cabota, his Italian name), a Venetian, and his son, Sebastian, under a commission granted by Henry VII of England, sailed from Bristol...and discovered Newfoundland on the 24th of June, 1497, near Cape Bonavista, and to which they gave the name of Terra Primum Vista, the land first seen (happy sight or view), because this was the place that first met their eyes in looking from the sea (Tocque, 1877).

The main purpose of this book is to re-examine John Cabot's voyages and their long-term significance, and to assess perceptions and sequels: What was the contemporary view of the importance of Cabot's discoveries? When did Europeans realize that what Columbus and Cabot had found was (to them) a New World? Finally, the book examines how the Cabots have been portrayed in legend, verse and painting.

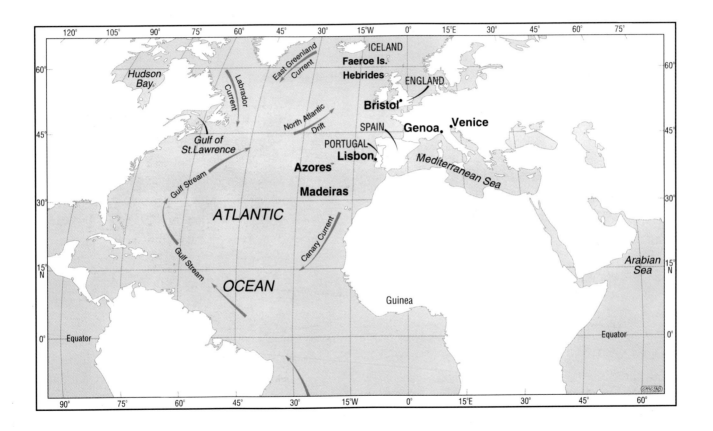

Most general history books give Christopher Columbus the credit for 'discovering' the New World, because he was the first modern European to find land on the western side of the Atlantic after a 70-day voyage across unknown seas (1492). His four voyages are well-documented, and they led directly to other Spanish discoveries and explorations, and to European settlement in Central and South America. But on his first and second (1493) voyages Columbus explored only the Caribbean islands, not the mainland. He thought Cuba was the territory of the Grand Khan, and called Haiti 'Hispaniola' because it resembled Spain. On his third voyage (1498) he cruised the Venezuelan coast, and on his fourth voyage (1502) touched the east coast of Central America from present-day Honduras to Panama.

Those who stress the significance of John Cabot's voyages claim that he may well have landed on the coast of mainland North America (which Columbus never saw), and also sighted and perhaps landed in Newfoundland in 1497, some time before Columbus encountered the mainland of South America (in 1498). But there are also those who believe that both Columbus and Cabot were preceded by other Europeans.

Illustration of a character from the dramatic work *Hysckescorner,* 1510, who claims to have travelled to Newfoundland.

here are a number of legends about pre-Columbian Atlantic crossings. Most cannot be backed or corroborated by the evidence of artifacts, and sometimes alleged remains have been found to be fakes. For instance, a stone with 'Carthaginian lettering' was found in Brazil in 1899, which described the sufferings of a group which had fled from the Roman destruction of Carthage in 146 BCE. In our own time, it has been claimed that Jewish refugees fled the Romans in the first century CE and sailed to America, where their blood mixed with that of the aboriginal inhabitants, an idea which springs from James Adair's *The History of the American Indian* (1775). The notion was revived by the 'find' of a bracelet made of brass (unknown to the early Indians) and 'confirmed' by an inscription on a Tennessee tombstone which – it is alleged – said 'Only for the Judaeans' in paleo-Hebrew.

A more familiar legend is that of St. Brendan, who was born in Ireland about 485, and founded a monastery at Clonfert, Galway. Over 70 years of age, he embarked with his brother monks on a westward voyage in a curragh, a large leather boat. Brendan's seven-year long adventure was set down in the *Navigatio Sancti Brendani Abbatis* in the tenth century. By island-hopping across the northern North Atlantic, could Brendan have reached Newfoundland? It has been reported that at Griquet, on Newfoundland's Northern Peninsula, a nine ton rock bore inscriptions in what some said was Ogham, the ancient alphabet of the Celtic priest-class (McGhee and Tuck, 1977).

There is nothing inherently impossible in any of these legends. Sailing the open ocean west of the 'Pillars of Hercules' might well have been difficult, however, as primitive vessels could only go with the wind, and it would seem that prevailing westerlies would have prevented a curragh from leaving the Irish coast. Yet Scandinavian settlers encountered Irish Christian hermits in Iceland in the ninth century, which shows that a leather boat, island-hopping between Ireland, the Hebrides, Faroe and Iceland, could make such a journey by waiting for good weather. In 1976 Tim Severin left Brandon, Ireland, in a curragh, hoping to show that St. Brendan could have reached the New World. He landed near Musgrave Harbour, Newfoundland, 13 months later (Severin, 1978).

(left) St. Brendan and his monks encounter a siren.
(right) Their ship is attacked by a sea monster.

he Viking adventure in North America is in a different category from the Brendan story. Firm evidence is provided by the Icelandic sagas of the 12th and 13th centuries, and by modern archaeological investigations. Eiric the Red, a Norwegian, explored and colonised coastal Greenland during the 980s, and at about the same time, an Icelander, Bjarni Herjolfsson, sighted unknown lands to the south and west. Leif Eiriksson explored these regions around 1000, beginning with land on the west side of Davis Strait.

According to the sagas, the Norse found and named three areas: Helluland, which is usually associated with Baffin Island; Markland, probably southern Labrador; and Vinland, whose location remains uncertain, some arguing for L'Anse aux Meadows on the northern tip of Newfoundland, where Norse remains have been found (Ingstad, 1969), others for places further south (Meldgaard, 1961). Another view is that Vinland was a general name for the whole area south of Markland, not a specific place. Whatever the truth of the matter, the knowledge of what Leif and others had found seems to have been lost. In Daniel Boorstin's words, 'What they did in America did not change their own or anybody else's view of the world...There was practically no feedback from the Vinland voyages'. In effect, the Norse reached North America, but did not *discover* it (Boorstin, 1983).

Why was this? The expeditions to North America were based on Norse settlements in Greenland, which in turn depended on links with Iceland and northern Europe. Over time these links became increasingly tenuous, and the Greenland settlements became almost totally isolated, virtually forgotten, their inhabitants facing the arrival of Thule Culture Inuit from the west. By the 15th century they were dying out (Jones, 1964).

Did Columbus or Cabot know about these voyages? There has been a great deal of speculation on this point. Some have suggested that Columbus, or perhaps Bristol mariners, may have seen evidence of the Norse voyages on a portolan (sailor's chart). But no such chart has ever been found and, until 1957, it was possible to say that there were no medieval maps of any origin purporting to show the northeast corner of North America. Then the apparently mid-15th century 'Vinland Map' emerged from a private collection. It showed the Old World in a conventional way, but also outlined a land-mass to the west which possibly represented the coast between Hudson Bay and the St. Lawrence (Skelton, Marston and Painter, 1965, 1995). A legend (text) on the map records the finding of 'Vinlandia Insula' by Bjarni and Leif. No earlier or later maps show the region in the same way, and the Vinland Map's authenticity has been hotly debated (Crone, 1966; Davies, 1966; Taylor, 1974; Quinn, in Story, 1982).

While some scholars are now prepared to accept that the Vinland Map is genuine, there is nevertheless a consensus that neither Columbus nor Cabot knew about the Norse voyages, even though Columbus may have visited Iceland (McManis, 1969; Quinn, 1992). It is virtually certain that neither of them had any idea that the Americas existed. In other words, the trail goes cold: we have confronted a discontinuity between the medieval and the modern world, and we must begin again.

A sea dragon

ith no certain knowledge of what lay to the west, medieval Europeans used their imagination, filling the unknown sea with islands, their existence and names based on legend and tradition. In classical times, Plato described Atlantis, a city submerged by the sea, and Seneca taught of the existence of a great continent which would one day appear beyond the ultimate limits of Thule (Iceland). The Irish legends brought islands such as St. Brendan's and Brasil, the Isle of the Blessed, imagined as more fruitful than anywhere else. The Island of the Seven Cities was supposed to be where bishops from the Iberian peninsula had taken refuge from the Moors. The mysterious island of Antillia first appeared on a map in 1424. Most medieval sailors felt about the Atlantic as had the 12th century Arab geographer Al-Idrisi: 'No one knows what is in that sea, because of many obstacles to navigation – profound darkness, high waves, frequent storms, innumerable monsters which people it, and violent winds. No sailor dares to penetrate it; they limit themselves to sailing along the coasts without losing sight of land'.

It was the Portuguese who began the exploration of the Atlantic in the 15th century, probing south along the West African coast. Their motives were mixed: economic ambition combined with geographical curiosity, a desire to spread Christianity, and a determination to continue the crusade against Islam by finding and allying with the mythical Prester John, a Christian king thought to live in Africa. The Portuguese had reached the Canary Islands as early as 1341. By 1420 they had planted their first settlements in the Madeiras, and they discovered the eastern Azores in 1427. They reached Guinea (modern Ghana) in 1470. Bartholomew Diaz rounded the Cape of Good Hope in 1488, and ten years later Vasco da Gama reached Calicut, India. The Portuguese might not have found Prester John, but they had found their own route to Asia and its lucrative trade in spices, silks and other exotic goods.

Ships returning home from the west African coast – where the Portuguese traded for gold, pepper and slaves – used the 'Guinea tack', a manoeuvre whereby they left the coast with northwest winds until they entered the zone of variable winds, where they set a course east for Portugal. As the Portuguese became more confident, the return was made by an even wider sweep westwards on the equatorial current, returning home through the Azores. This development reflected increasingly sophisticated navigational skills, as well as changes in the build and rig of vessels which made them more versatile.

Some mariners began to explore towards the west, the first being Diego de Teive, who in 1452 searched beyond the known islands of the Azores and discovered Flores and Corvo (Morison, 1940). Some Portuguese scholars claim he sighted land further to the west, which could have been Newfoundland (Cortesao, 1937). There were other voyages, of which little is known. One of particular interest was a search in 1473-74 for 'new islands and continents in the north' using routes pioneered by the Norse. The initiative, and probably the pilot, came from Portugal; the voyage was organized by the king of Denmark, and was led by German captains in his service. Joao Corte Real, the likely pilot, was rewarded with a governorship in the Azores for having discovered 'Stockfish Land'. Could this have been Newfoundland? (Larsen, 1925; da Mota, 1965).

It seems clear that the Portuguese believed that new lands lay to the west, and that rumours of discovery spread about Atlantic ports from Bergen to the Algarve. The rumours may have stimulated the men of Bristol, and were probably known to Columbus, who was acquainted with Corte Real's sons. But were they perceived as genuinely new lands, or as part of Asia? The latter is more probable, and mariners began actively to plan to reach Asia by sailing west.

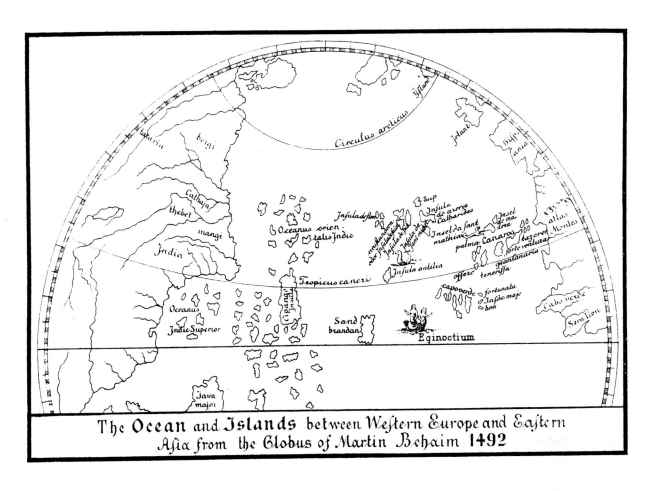

The Atlantic Ocean after Martin Behaim's globe, 1492. Real islands off West Africa, imaginary islands in mid-ocean and Cipango (Japan), Cathaja (Cathay: China) and India. (Maine Historical Society).

his was an old idea whose time had come. In 1474 the Florentine cosmographer Toscanelli wrote a famous letter to Alfonso V of Portugal. It displayed Toscanelli's knowledge of the travels to the Orient by Marco Polo and others, and explained how to find Asia by sailing west, a route which he thought would be much shorter than rounding Africa. First, he wrote, one would reach Antillia, then the rich island of Cipango and, finally, by a short sail, the Asian mainland of the Grand Khan. This was nine years before Columbus made his own, rejected, submission to the Portuguese king on the same lines.

Educated Europeans had known that the world was round since the time of Eratosthenes (275-194 BCE). Aristotle believed that 'the ocean between Spain and India is small', as did Strabo writing in the time of Christ. Seneca thought the ocean between Europe and India could be traversed in a few days, and Pliny was certain that it was but a 'short sail' eastward from the Arabian Gulf to Spain. Fifteenth century minds might not have believed that the world was so small, but their geographical ideas were still dominated by the second century Alexandrian, Ptolemy, and limited to Eurasia and an incomplete Africa surrounded by the 'Ocean Sea'. By the 1490s, the westerly sea route to China and Japan was apparent to anyone who examined Martin Behaim's globe, on which the easternmost and westernmost known lands were separated by only about 120 degrees of sea. Ptolemy had estimated the earth's circumference to be about 18,000 miles and Columbus used this figure to calculate how long it would take him to reach Asia by sailing west. He also accepted the hypothesis that six-sevenths of the earth's surface was land, derived from *Imago Mundi*, a world geography written in 1410 from ideas generated long before. Columbus concluded that Cipango was only 2,963 miles from Spain. Had he known that the distance was nearer 12,000 miles, he would never have set sail.

Born in Genoa in 1451, Columbus learned navigation in the Mediterranean. In 1476 he joined a Genoan fleet trading to England. Wrecked off Cape St. Vincent, he settled in Lisbon and married a Portuguese whose father knew the Atlantic islands. He lived on Madeira, then returned to Lisbon where the Atlantic charts he acquired from his Portuguese relations stimulated his work as a chart-maker. He knew the Portuguese footholds in West Africa, and probably visited Bristol in 1479. His son claimed he had also been in Iceland, a place where Bristolians traded (Morison, 1942).

Which brings us to Cabot. While Columbus was learning the methods of Portuguese navigation, another Italian with the same persistence and ambition was gaining experience in Italy and Iberia, and obviously knew about the western approaches to England.

A narwhale

A. Williamson remarked that it was strange that we know so little about John Cabot and his voyages compared to Christopher Columbus. The reason, he thought, was that 'Columbus had a faithful friend, the Bishop Las Casas [his biographer], and a son who revered his father's memory and saved it from being forgotten. John Cabot, on the other hand, had a son, Sebastian, who seems to have been jealous of his father's fame and to have done his best to destroy the memory of his achievements' (Williamson, 1925). While he might have added that Columbus was a relentless self-publicist, Williamson was essentially correct. John Cabot became subsumed by his prominent and long-lived son Sebastian (Almagia, 1958), who was for centuries accepted as the discoverer. Playing safe, early historians of Bristol gave the credit to 'John Sebastian Cabot'.

Giovanni (or Zuan) Caboto was probably born in Gaeta, near Naples, around 1455, but was brought up in Genoa (Gallo, 1948). He was therefore of the same generation and city as Columbus. He later moved to Venice, and was granted citizenship in 1476 (Biggar, 1911; Williamson, 1962; Skelton, 1966). He married Mattea about 1482; their children were Ludovico, Sebastiano and Sancio. Cabot made his living as a merchant, trading to Alexandria for Asian spices, dyes and silks.

In about 1490 he moved to Valencia, Spain. Becoming known as a cartographer and navigator, he approached officials in Seville and Lisbon with plans for a westward voyage to Cathay. It is not known 'where or how his quest crossed that of Columbus, who from before 1485 had been engaged in a similar quest' (Quinn, 1993). In any event, he was unsuccessful; and Columbus' triumph in 1492 meant that his chances of Spanish royal patronage were non-existent. Cabot turned to England, and by 1495 he was living in Bristol. Two linked questions follow: Why England? and why Bristol?

Cabot was evidently obsessed by the idea of finding a western route to Asia. Spain now thought it had its route, discovered by Columbus, and Portugal was preoccupied by the southern route to India, around Africa. Moreover, Spain and Portugal had signed the Treaty of Tordesillas in 1494, which awarded all non-Christian lands west of a north-south line drawn west of the Cape Verde Islands to Spain, and those lands to the east of the line to Portugal. This division of the world seemed to cut England out of the competition, and was certainly of concern to Henry VII – who had in the past refused financial help to Columbus, a decision he may have come to regret. Cabot could offer a second chance, a northern, English route, and the opportunity for England to stake claims, in spite of the treaty, in an area where neither Spain nor Portugal was especially active. England seemed to present the best chance for royal patronage.

Cabot was obviously also optimistic that he would find financial backing. He had probably made contact with Bristol merchants while in Spain (Ballesteros-Gaibros, 1943), and this may have influenced his decision to move to one of the great trading ports of late medieval England, one of the wealthiest towns in the country. Bristol merchants exported wool, tin, lead, cloth and other merchandise to Ireland, northern Europe, France and Spain, bringing back wine, olive oil and other goods. Their ships sailed as far south as the Azores, and as far north as Iceland, where they traded in fish (Carus-Wilson, 1962). Bristol was 'the outpost of English Atlantic endeavour' (Ryan, 1996). But why would Bristol merchants have wanted to back a risky venture into the western ocean?

The usual answer has been that these merchants were looking for new sources of fish. For much of the 15th century Bristol had been active, together with other ports, in the Iceland trade, exchanging wood, grain and other items for stockfish[1], which was sold in England and southern Europe. There had been problems with this trade for some years, and by the 1480s Bristol merchants were being squeezed out by the German Hanseatic League. New sources of supply were needed. This reasoning has been used to help explain why Bristol ships were probing the Atlantic before Cabot arrived – indeed, some have gone so far as to argue that

Newfoundland and its banks had already been discovered (Quinn, 1961; Forbes Taylor, 1976).

In 1480 John Jay went in search of the island of 'Brazylle', but failed to find anything during a nine-week voyage. The next year, two ships left, again 'to search and fynde a certain isle called the Isle of Brasile' (Quinn, 1935), and the fact that they carried salt has suggested to some that they were looking for fish (Ryan, 1996). In July 1498, writing to the Spanish monarchs from London, Pedro de Ayala noted that 'For the last seven years the people of Bristol have equipped two, three, four caravels to go in search of the island of Brazil and the Seven Cities'. In another letter, John Day, a merchant in the Spanish trade, reporting to Columbus on Cabot's 1497 voyage, mentioned that it was 'considered certain that the cape of the said land [found by Cabot] was found and discovered in the past by the men of Bristol who found Brasil as your Lordship well knows. It was called the Island of Brasil and it is assumed and believed to be the mainland that the men from Bristol found'. (Vigneras, 1956; Ruddock, 1966). Much later, in 1527, Robert Thorne claimed that his father, also Robert, and Hugh Eliot, both Bristol merchants, were the true 'discoverers of the New Founde Landes'. Much later still, the Elizabethan scholar John Dee said the date was 1494.

There is also cartographic evidence. The rearrangement of Atlantic islands on maps drawn in the 1490s and the nature of their coastlines, combined with other documentary evidence, has suggested to some that Bristol men could have found Newfoundland, calling it Brasil or Seven Cities (Quinn, 1961; Taylor, 1964).

This evidence is suggestive but not conclusive. All that can be said is that ships from Bristol were probing the north Atlantic in the years before 1497, and may have reached Newfoundland and Labrador. But the motivation was unlikely to have been fish. Bristol merchants, it has been argued, were not so much interested in catching fish as in trading it, and also in a secure return on investment. These were inexpensive, small-scale expeditions, which were really speculations: they might, conceivably, find the Asian jackpot (McGrath, 1978).

abot's scheme was to find a shorter, northern route to Asia which would evade the division of the world between Spain and Portugal. He was, in a sense, the first advocate of what was later known as the Northwest Passage, and his impact on the English court was probably considerable. Certainly, there had been no talk in England of a North Atlantic route to Asia before Cabot arrived (Williamson, 1962).

Cabot petitioned Henry VII for permission to sail with the participation of the merchants of Bristol, and he received letters patent on 5 March, 1496. In the petition (in English), the Cabots are called 'John Cabotto, Citezen of Venice, Lewes, Sebastyan and Soncio, his sonnys'. In the patent (in Latin), the Cabots, with their heirs and deputies (unnamed Bristol merchants), are given authority to use five ships, and to sail to all parts of 'the eastern, western and northern sea', to discover and investigate 'whatsoever islands, countries, regions or provinces of heathens and infidels, in whatsoever part of the world placed, which before this time were unknown to all Christians'.

This meant that Cabot (on behalf of the English Crown) would respect Spain's right to what Columbus had discovered; but if he was the first in other regions, England had the prior right. Henry VII could not foresee the Spanish empire which would develop in America. He saw only 'a Spanish attempt which seemed substantially to have failed (Columbus's crude islands, his men straggling back from the Indies without the expected loot), a new and better solution offered to himself, and a common-sense proposal that each should take and enjoy what he could find' (Williamson, 1962). The new discoveries were to be occupied in the king's name, and he would receive one-fifth of the profits. The grantees would be exempt from paying customs on goods brought back to Bristol.

It used to be thought that the 1497 voyage was Cabot's first from Bristol, but the discovery in 1956 of John Day's letter to Columbus (mentioned above), a highly significant event in Cabot scholarship, proved that there had been an earlier voyage in 1496. That spring, therefore, Cabot would have been busily exercising his right (by the patent) to get all subjects of the king to render assistance in fitting out his ship and buying stores and victuals. Presumably, Bristol merchants supported him and a Bristol crew was enlisted. All we know about the 1496 voyage is in the Day letter: 'Since your lordship wants information relating to the first voyage, here is what happened: he [Cabot] went with one ship, he had a disagreement with his crew, he was short of food and ran into bad weather, and he decided to turn back'. Was the ship prepared in a hurry, poorly victualled, and with a crew laid on instead of selected? Or perhaps this was a trial voyage, testing both vessel and crew? We do not know, either, when Cabot's storm-damaged ship regained Bristol, or how failure (if this is what it was) was handled.

Woodcut of sea monsters inhabiting the North Atlantic, Sebastian Münster *Cosmographia,* 1550.

Eve of Departure. Painting by Donald McCleod, 1995. © Cabot Heritage Ltd.

abot's ship was probably called the *Matthew* after his Venetian wife, Mattea. There is no record of this vessel in the Bristol customs records in 1492-3, and there is no further list of ships using the port until 1503-4. It seems almost certain that it was built in Bristol not long before Cabot won his letters patent. We do not know if the *Matthew* was employed in the first voyage. If it was, the poor performance of ship and crew might have been the result of both being green, the ship itself not yet properly trimmed and ballasted. It was described later as a 'navicula', meaning a ship of the smaller sort, such as a bark, of 50 'toneles', one able to carry 50 'tuns' of wine or other cargo, with a fathom draught.

The *Matthew* had flush decks, a high sterncastle and three masts, like the Portuguese caravel. Her oaken keel would have been laid on wooden blocks and her framework made from templates. Beams were laid across the ribs and strengthened with 'knees'. Deck and side planking was pegged into place, made watertight with hemp and tar and painted in bright colours. Sea trials would have followed in the Bristol Channel. The square mainsails on the two forward masts propelled the vessel in a following wind; the lateen sail on the rear mast was rigged in the same direction as the keel, helping the vessel sail into the wind. The whole ship would have been made with timbers brought down the Rivers Severn and Wye from the great forests of Wyre and Dean[2].

When Columbus departed from Palos, Andalusia, at dawn on 3 August, 1492, with his famous three little ships, there was a vast crowd of spectators. Although Cabot's 1497 voyage also enjoyed royal favour, it was his second attempt. Would it therefore have attracted so much attention?

The sailors' church by the Quay was St. Stephen's, where the navigator Martin Pring, and the coloniser of Newfoundland, John Guy, would both be buried over 100 years later. It has been envisaged as the church from which, on a bright day in May, a procession of dignitaries led Cabot and crew to their ship (Little, 1983). An enduring image to Bristolians is Ernest Board's depiction (1908) of the *Matthew*'s departure with fanfares and heraldic devices, the sail already aloft like a flying carpet and Cabot dressed as if in a pageant. In 1947, the Newfoundlander Harold Goodridge also painted the departure scene with Church and State saying farewell, the great church of St. Mary Redcliffe serving as a backdrop (cover).

Such a sendoff probably never happened, and it is likely that the epic voyage started on a muted note. There were about 20 on board: Cabot, a Genoese barber (surgeon), a Burgundian, two Bristol merchants, assumed to be Robert Thorne and Hugh Elyot (who, as mentioned above, were later claimed as the 'the discoverers of the New Founde Landes'), and Bristol sailors. Whether one or more of Cabot's sons were on the voyage is not known, though Sebastian later claimed to have been a participant.

Model of the *Matthew*, now in the Newfoundland Museum, made in 1947 by Ernest Maunder for the Newfoundland Historical Society.

Photograph: Ned Pratt.

ow did Cabot sail over 4,000 miles and find his way home? In the Arab world, from which so much was learned by the West, pilots were classified as coastal, intermediate and master. The coastal pilot stayed in sight of known landmarks. The intermediate pilot could strike out on a fixed course and make his chosen destination using the compass. The master pilot was different: he was not expected to lose his bearings, even when obliged to make changes of course when out of sight of land. He instinctively watched tides, winds, water depth and colour. These, with signs like the direct flight of migrating birds, could extend the horizon. In addition, master pilots could use the sun and the stars, measuring latitude with a variety of instruments.

It was Cabot's skill as an advanced navigator that would have persuaded Bristolians that he should command the *Matthew*. He would have had an astrolabe, charts, a cross-staff, a nocturnal and a traverse board, as well as a notebook of mathematical tables. Most of these instruments measured the angle between the stars or the sun, and the horizon, in order to work out the ship's position. While the astrolabe was difficult to use on a rolling ship, the less accurate cross-staff, which measured the angle of a star in relation to the horizon, could be substituted. Cabot could also use the nocturnal to measure the position of Ursa Major or Minor in relation to the Pole star.

Out of sight of land, Cabot could estimate latitude, but had difficulty with longitude (how far west of his starting point he had reached). His compass, too, would have given him problems, since the declination[3] increased as he sailed west: 'going so far out [into the Atlantic]' wrote John Day, 'his compass needle failed to point north and marked two rhumbs[4] below'. Years later, Sebastian Cabot puzzled over the compass variations he found in the Atlantic. He knew it was zero at the Azores and close to 22.5 degrees at Cape Race, and so came to the conclusion that the variation altered with the meridian. This was false, but he saw in this a method of finding longitude 'and hugged what he thought was a valuable secret to the day of his death' (Taylor, 1963).

A cross-staff.

abot's own record of his voyage has disappeared and his crew left no accounts. The only information comes from non-participants – three letters from two foreign agents in England, Raimondo de Soncino and Lorenzo Pasqualigo, long known, and the John Day letter, discovered in the mid-20th century (Vigneras, 1956). We can usefully extract their information about the voyage as follows, drawing from translations printed by leading scholars (Biggar, 1911; Vigneras, 1957; Williamson, 1962):

Lorenzo Pasqualigo, London, to his brothers in Venice, 23 August, 1497 (Venice, Biblioteca Marciana) – *The Venetian ('Zuam Talbot') has discovered 'mainland 700 leagues away'; 'he coasted it for 300 leagues and landed and did not see any person'; [he] 'planted on the land which he has found a large cross with a banner of England and one of St. Mark'; he was 'three months on the voyage; and this is certain'; 'On the way back he saw two islands, but was unwilling to land ... as he was in want of provisions'.*

Attributed to Raimondo de Soncino (Milanese ambassador in England) to the Duke of Milan, 24 August, 1497 (Milan Archives) – *'...a Venetian...has found two very large and fertile new islands. He has also discovered the Seven Cities, 400 leagues from England, on the western passage'.*

Raimondo de Soncino, London, to the Duke of Milan, 18 December, 1497 (Milan Archives) – *'Zoane Caboto...passed Ireland...and then bore towards the north...leaving the north on his right hand after some days...at length arrived at*

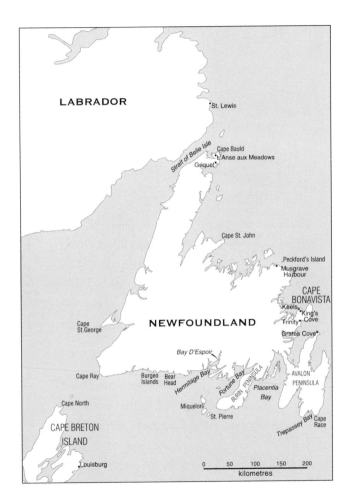

the mainland, where he hoisted the royal standard and took possession for the king...'; 'in a map, and also in a solid sphere...[he]...shows where he has been. In going towards the east he passed far beyond the country of the Tanais'.

John Day, in Spain, to the Lord Grand Admiral, undated (December 1497- January 1498, Archivo General de Simancas) – 'I am sending ...a copy of the land which he has found. I do not send the map because I am not satisfied with it...from the said copy your Lordship will learn what you wish to know, for in it are named the capes of the mainland and the islands, and thus you will see where land was first sighted, since most of the land was discovered after turning back...the cape nearest to Ireland is 1,800 miles west of Dursey Head which is in Ireland, and the southernmost part of the Island of the Seven Cities is west of Bordeaux River...he landed at only one spot of the mainland, near the place where land was first sighted...with a crucifix and raised banners'. 'They left England towards the *end of May, and must have been on the way 35 days before sighting land; the wind was east-north-east and the sea calm going and coming back, except for...a storm two or three days before finding land; and going so far out, his compass needle failed to point north and marked two rhumbs below. They spent about a month discovering the coast and from the above mentioned cape of the mainland which is nearest to Ireland, they returned to the coast of Europe in fifteen days. They had the wind behind them, and he reached Brittany because the sailors confused him, saying that he was heading too far north. From there he came to Bristol, and he went to see the King...'.*

There is very little more in the whole record relating to this voyage except dates for the beginning and end of it set down in various chronicles, which may not be reliable, and maps made in succeeding years which incorporate Cabot's own lost information. What is most remarkable is the paucity of knowledge about the voyage;

it is not first-hand, and all those who retailed their land-fall theories before the Day letter was found had only a dozen lines to use. As a result, it is impossible to say with absolute certainty where John Cabot sailed. All that historians can do is to take the available evidence, and try to construct a reasonable hypothesis. What follows is one such attempt.

sing the documentary evidence – and leaving aside maps for the moment – how well can we reconstruct the voyage, adding our knowledge of 15th century navigation methods, and what we believe to have been the effect of wind and weather on a westerly voyage in summer?

The voyage can be broken down into four segments: the Atlantic crossing; the landfall; coasting; and the return. This will help us understand why there have been so many different interpretations. It is difficult to separate these segments, and some scholars do not begin their reconstructions from the beginning. Generally, however, all those who have speculated about the voyage try to find fixed points of best evidence, around which other circumstances may be fitted to build a hypothesis.

THE ATLANTIC CROSSING AND THE LANDFALL

The first divergence of opinion is whether Cabot left Bristol in early or late May – modern scholars, using the Day letter, tend to favour the second alternative (Jackson, 1963). That aside, it is generally agreed that Cabot would have sailed down the Bristol Channel, across to Fastnet, and then north along the Irish coast before turning west. But how far? This is a matter of great importance, since once out of sight of land navigators sailed by latitude. It is often assumed that Cabot's point of departure was Dursey Head (51°31' N), since it was mentioned by John Day, but this is not universally accepted. Harrisse (1892), selected Valencia (51°50' N) on the basis of the number of days taken to cross the Atlantic. Dawson (1897) thought Cabot would have gone as far north as 53° N in order to get as close to Asia as he could, according to the maps at his disposal. For similar reasons, Jackson (1963) argued that Achill Head (54° 04' N) is the most likely place.

A northerly departure is probable, but could Cabot have drifted off course? Dawson and Clements Markham (1893) thought that currents and magnetic variations affecting his compass could have pulled him as much as 200 miles south. Modern scholars, with access to the Day letter and a greater knowledge of 15th century navigational techniques, tend to think that Cabot would have kept more or less on course. He was familiar with the phenomenon of compass variation, kept the North Star on his right, had instruments with which to check latitude, and had ways to measure, if only approximately, how far west he had travelled.

And how far did he travel on the crossing? Pasqualigo reported it was 700 leagues from England to the landfall. Day said it was 1,800 *millas* from the landfall to Ireland. These distances translate into 1,826 nautical miles and 1,400 nautical miles respectively, and appear to be underestimates. Soncino stated that Cabot had 'passed far beyond the country of the Tanais', meaning Tartary or Cathay, which Jackson interprets to mean more than 1,800 nautical miles.

To distance must be added the time taken. Day said the passage took 35 days. If the first five took Cabot to the Irish coast, 30 are left to cross the Atlantic. Assuming that the *Matthew* could sail within six points of the wind at five knots, Jackson added seasonally expected winds in nine consecutive zones, and reckoned that Cabot could have crossed the Atlantic from Ireland in just under 24 days, nearly 36 days in all. The currents would have reduced his latitude from about 54° N to 53° N or 52° N. This brings Cabot to the south coast of Labrador, in the area of Cape Lewis (52°22' N). If Cabot had checked his observations, he would have found that he was approximately in the latitude of Dursey Head, 1,800 *millas* to the east.

COASTING AND RETURN

The landfall occurred on 24 June, and Cabot was back in Bristol on 6 August, after a 15 day crossing from the easternmost cape 'of the mainland' he had discovered. He therefore explored the region for about a month. Pasqualigo said Cabot coasted 700 leagues, and Day stated that he sailed as far south as the parallel

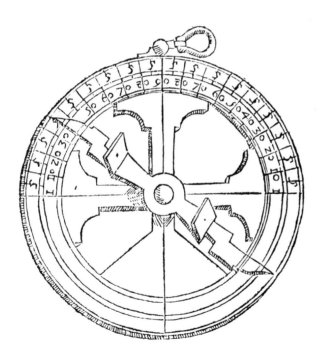

An astrolabe.

of the Bordeaux river, approximately 45°35' N. Day also said that most of land was discovered on the way back to England. So where did Cabot go?

Jackson argues that from Labrador, Cabot would have sailed south and west, since that was the direction in which he thought Cathay was located. He entered the Straits of Belle Isle, and choosing the eastern shore because it looked like mainland, reached Cape Ray. Here the land swung abruptly to the east, and Cabot would have realised that he had found an island which, because it was not large enough to be Cipango, had to be the Island of the Seven Cities, mentioned by most sources. At Cape Race he sailed north to regain a latitude near to that he had taken from Ireland, turning east near Fogo and reaching Brittany before returning to Bristol.

he literary evidence describing the landfall comes only from the same 'reporters' as before:

Pasqualigo, 23 August, 1497 – '... he landed and did not see any person; but he has brought here (to London) to the king certain snares which were spread to take game and a needle for making nets, and he found certain notched (or felled) trees so that by this he judges that there are inhabitants. Being in doubt he returned to his ship...and he says that the tides are slack and do not run as they do here'.

Soncino, 18 December, 1497 – After taking possession, they took 'certain tokens'; 'They say that the land is excellent and temperate, and they believe that Brazil wood and silk are native there. They assert that the sea is swarming with fish which can be taken not only with the net, but in baskets let down with a stone...'.

Day, undated (December 1497/January 1498) – 'Since he was with just a few people, he did not dare advance inland beyond the shooting distance of a crossbow, and after taking in fresh water he returned to his ship. All along the coast they found many fish like those which in Iceland are dried in the open and sold in England and other countries, and these are called in English stockfish; and thus following the shore they saw two forms running on land one after the other, but they could not tell if they were human beings or animals; and it seemed to them that there were fields where they thought might also be villages, and they saw a forest whose foliage looked beautiful'.

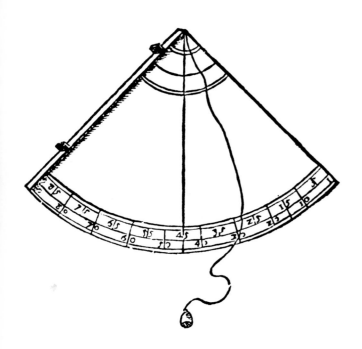

A quadrant.

Day also stated that Cabot 'landed at only one spot of the mainland, near the place where land was first sighted...'. There is nothing more. If we put it all together, Cabot and his men went ashore, the first Europeans since the Norse (Englishmen led by an Italian) to set foot in North America. They put up a cross and planted beside it the banners of England and Venice, thus claiming the country for the king of England. They met no inhabitants, but saw signs of human life. Cabot thought he had reached the north-eastern extremity of Asia and, like Columbus, thought the populous cities with roofs of gold, and the sources of silk and spices, could not be too far off.

ackson's reconstruction of the 1497 voyage, outlined above, is one of many, and does not rely on cartographic evidence. Moreover, Jackson was neither a Canadian nor a Newfoundlander – a factor which should not be discounted, since in controversial matters like the Cabot landfall, patriotism has had a definite impact on interpretation. Before 1949, when Newfoundland joined Canada, Canadian scholars tended to rely on cartography to argue for a landfall on Cape Breton Island.

Although several maps indicate Cabot's landfall, all are very late except for the La Cosa map of about 1500. Found in 1832, it is the earliest map to represent any part of the North American continent[5]. It is a large planisphere of the entire known world, in colour on ox-hide, with the western, trans-Atlantic part depicted on a larger scale than the Old World. It was made by Juan de la Cosa, a skilled Biscayan navigator who sailed with Columbus, and shows the discoveries of both Columbus and Cabot: the former's 'Indies', and the latter's 'north-eastern part of Asia'. It is probable that Cabot's own chart of his voyage (later lost) was passed by the Spanish ambassador in London to the king in Spain, and it is also possible that La Cosa received information about Cabot's third voyage by the same channel (Nunn, 1943).

Both Biggar (1911) and Ganong (1929; in Ganong 1964) were convinced of the importance of La Cosa; they were supported by Williamson and Skelton (Williamson, 1962), who considered it 'the only map which unambiguously illustrates John Cabot's voyage of 1497 and – with less certainty – his voyage of 1498'. The most remarkable aspect of the 'north-eastern coast' on La Cosa is that it is marked by place names and a line of five English flags. These are the map-maker's flags, but some suggest that they are places where

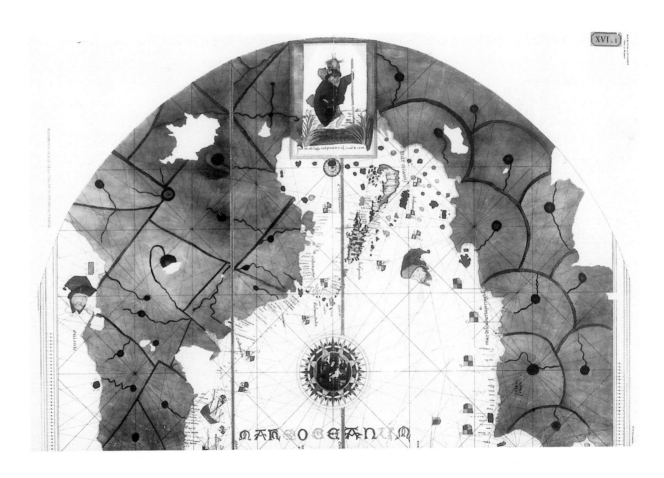

Mappamunde of Juan de la Cosa, 1500. La Cosa showed both Columbus' and Cabot's discoveries.
National Map Collection, National Archives of Canada, #10030.

Cabot (like Gilbert at St. John's, 1583, and Cartier at Gaspé, 1534) claimed the land for the Crown. At one place, La Cosa locates 'Cauo de ynglaterra' (Cape of England) and over the sea he writes 'mar de descubierta por inglese' (sea discovered by the English).

Where is this coast, was it straight, and did it appear to Cabot to lie east-west? There is a range of answers in the literature. It has been identified as the north shore of the St. Lawrence, the south coast of Newfoundland from Cape Race westwards (including Cape Breton Island), and as the coast from Cape Breton to the Bay of Fundy. Still others thought that what was mapped east-west should really have been north-south, so that the line of flags stretched from Cape Chidley (near Hudson Strait), either to Cape Race or to Cape Breton. All these interpretations differ markedly from that of Jackson.

The great cartographic scholar William Ganong (1864-1941), a New Brunswicker, performed an analysis of the La Cosa map which has been called 'one of the most brilliant "old map" expositions ever written' (Layng, in Ganong, 1964). Assuming the flagged area was constructed from Cabot information, the problem was to identify the true coastlines. Ganong realised that the La Cosa map might be a simplification of Cabot's own map, the result of successive re-drawings, and also believed that it was made with compasses corrected for the very different declination in Europe, 'the effect of which was to throw our coasts out of line in the way shown by Cosa'. He concluded that the named coast was more consistent with Cape Race to Cape Breton than with any other interpretation.

Ganong thought that Cabot missed Newfoundland on the outward voyage, made a landfall on Cape Breton, and then returned along Newfoundland's south coast. Between the third and fourth flags is written 'Cauo Descubierto' ([the] cape [that was] discovered); to Ganong, this had to be the landfall. The cape to the east is (in translation) the 'Cape of St. George', while to the west is the 'mar descubierta por iglese' (sea discovered by the English). The islands shown beneath this phrase

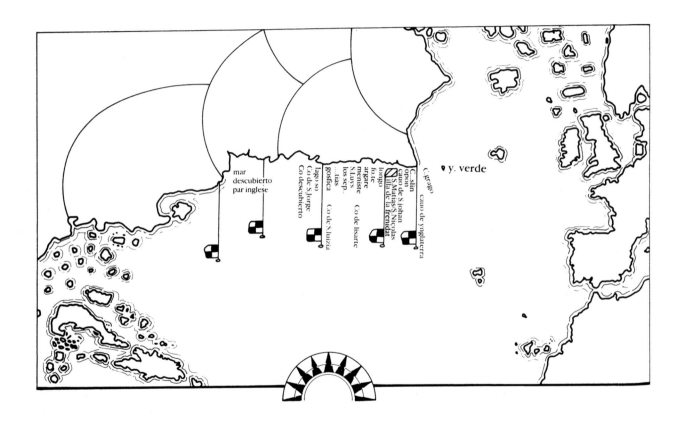

Flagged area of coastline accredited to the English, detail after Juan de la Cosa's map.
Taken from *The Columbus Myth* by Ian Wilson, published by Simon & Schuster. © Ian Wilson, 1991.

could be the way the mosaic of islands, peninsulas and broken country at the eastern end of Cape Breton Island looked from the sea. The fourth flag, Ganong thought, might mark the landing and the erection of marks of English possession at Louisbourg, a place called (in either English or French) 'English Harbour' until the early 18th century. Was it here, then, that Cabot erected his 'large cross with a banner of England and one of St. Mark'?

Ganong suggested that the 'bight' between flags three and four represented the great entrance to the Gulf of St. Lawrence (called Cabot Strait only since 1888). Both he and G.R.F. Prowse, a Newfoundlander, considered that the La Cosa 'Co. de s:Jorge' survived as Cape St. George, projecting into the Gulf on the Port au Port Peninsula of western Newfoundland, and could be the oldest authenticated place name of European origin not only in Newfoundland, but also in the entire North American continent. By this interpretation, then, after examining the Cape Breton coast, Cabot crossed to Newfoundland, mistaking the Gulf of St. Lawrence for a great bight of the coast with shore hidden by mist or distance (precisely as did Cartier 37 years later). Alternatively, Cabot might have thought the Gulf to be open sea, in which case, we have good explanation why he described the discovery as 'two new very large and fertile islands'.

Ganong then took Cabot along the southern coast of Newfoundland, the flags and place names marking Cape Ray, the Burgeo area ('Pisques'), where Cabot found the fishery so abundant, Bear Head ('Co.de Lisarte'), Cape La Hune ('Forte'), Hermitage Bay or Bay d'Espoir ('Ro.Longo'), St. Pierre and Miquelon ('Isla de la Trendar'), and the tip of the Burin Peninsula ('C. Fastanatre') where, also, the fifth flag records 'Cauo de ynglaterra' ('Cape of England').

This cape is the closest to England on La Cosa. What, then, is the prominent island off the east coast? This, wrote Ganong, was the way the southern tip of the Avalon might appear through the mists as Cabot tracked across Placentia Bay. In going over the same evidence, this is also how Leslie Harris interpreted it (Harris,

1967). Indeed, Pasqualigo's statement that 'on the way back he saw two islands' would fit well as, perhaps, the fog closed in on the *Matthew* about Trepassey Bay. Short of provisions, Cabot would continue eastward, for home.

By Ganong's reconstruction, then, Cabot was unlikely to have seen any part of Newfoundland north of Cape St. George in the west and Cape Race in the east. A similar path was followed by D.B. Quinn, but he suggested a course from Cape Breton stretched out to reach Cape Bauld (Quinn, 1977), a place where many scholars bring Cabot in from the Atlantic on his outward voyage (Harrisse, 1896; Morison, 1971).

The Cape Breton landfall may also be supported by the so-called 'Sebastian Cabot' or 'Paris' map of 1544, found in Germany in 1856. The map is printed with Spanish legends, which apparently contain Sebastian Cabot's personal information (Skelton, in Williamson, 1962). They indicate that the landfall was made on 24 June and that an adjacent island was named St. John. They add that the discovery was made by John Cabot and his son Sebastian, and ascribe the authorship of the map to Sebastian. The position of the words 'Prima Tierra Vista' indicates that Cape North, Cape Breton, was the approximate locality of the land first seen. The date of the landfall is corroborated by Toby's Chronicle of Bristol, but the map's reliability in other respects has been questioned (Williamson, 1962).

However, nearly all the proponents of a Cape Breton landfall – Markham, Tarducci, Thwaites, Bourinot, Dawson, Harvey, Biggar, Ganong, Burpee – regarded both the La Cosa and Sebastian Cabot/Paris maps as documentary evidence which supported their case. Even if the map is discounted, a case can still be made for a southern landfall, and the Day letter seems to have made little difference. Williamson, who wrote both before and after it was found, opted for Cape Breton in 1929 and for Maine (cautiously) in 1962, which is also favoured by Quinn (1993); and Vigneras, who found the Day letter, also argued for Cape Breton (Vigneras, 1957).

here is no doubt that great passions have been aroused in Newfoundland about the question of Cabot's landfall. The strongest local tradition is that he reached Cape Bonavista (with rather less attention being given to his subsequent coasting). We have seen that Philip Tocque accepted Bonavista, and the notion goes back at least to the map of Newfoundland prepared by Captain John Mason in about 1617 and published in several editions. This map contains many familiar place names on the English Shore. Over Cape Bonavista, called 'North Faulkland', is marked 'Bona Vista Caboto primum reperta'. Many believe that Mason, who was governor of the London and Bristol Company in Newfoundland for three and a half years, obtained information from an older chart now lost, or from West Country fishermen. Since this is the sole historical document to support a Bonavista landfall, it must be backed by the belief that some of the fishermen who knew Mason also knew the sons or grandsons of those who sailed with Cabot. As counterpoint, it could be claimed that Mason, and perhaps his informants too, adopted the Bonavista theory simply because they themselves took that place for their point of arrival and departure over the years.

To champion Bonavista as the landfall is sound enough, however, if the argument in support is sustained by latitude sailing from the mouth of the Bristol Channel, encountering those natural forces – currents and magnetic variation – which many scholars have suggested would tend to make Cabot's course swerve southwards. This is, in general, the line of argument taken by Fabian O'Dea in the most convincing modern article supporting the Bonavista landfall (O'Dea, 1988). He thinks it probable that Cabot sailed west from Fastnet, and was then carried south by the Labrador Current as he approached North America, a

The John Mason Map, 1617. National Map Collection, National Archives of Canada, # 21046.

point in the voyage when he also encountered a storm. Thus Bonavista emerges as a realistic landfall.

Another Newfoundlander who supported Bonavista, W. A. Munn, suggested that Mason deliberately placed the Cabot discovery claim over the cape in Latin because he 'wanted every map-maker in Spain, Portugal, France or Italy to understand the meaning correctly'; and he saw an immediate response, in that a French map by Du Pont of Dieppe (1625) called Cape Bonavista 'Primum Inventa' (first named). Munn scathingly dismissed the Cape Breton theorists, going so far as to claim that they had 'created a resentment from Newfoundlanders that Canadians have over-stepped the bounds of courtesy by asserting what they cannot prove' (Munn, 1936). O'Dea follows Munn in criticising the arguments in favour of Cape Breton, though less strenuously.

But with Bonavista as the landfall, one must still plot the coasting voyage. Munn argued that because Cabot was sailing west, he would have gone northwest, via the Northern Peninsula to southern Labrador and home. Munn was preoccupied with La Cosa, and located the cape at the fifth flag, the 'Cape of England', in Labrador. More recently, L.E.F. English considered that most of La Cosa's flag-waving coast was a representation of the east coast of Newfoundland, and brought Cabot to the Avalon Peninsula. Baccalieu Island was Cabot's 'Isle of St. John', or even the south-eastern portion of the Avalon, because coming south into Conception Bay 'this appears as an island'. Not wholeheartedly for Bonavista, English brought Cabot through the Narrows: 'There is a tradition that John Cabot entered the harbour of St. John's on the evening of June 24th' (English, 1962). O'Dea agreed that Cabot would have sailed south. However, the route that best fits the evidence, he thinks, has Cabot rounding Cape Race and possibly reaching Cape Breton, where he turned back to explore the coast more thoroughly.

One further map, neglected by many landfall theorists, is Gastaldi's of 1556. This still showed Newfoundland and Labrador as the familiar series of

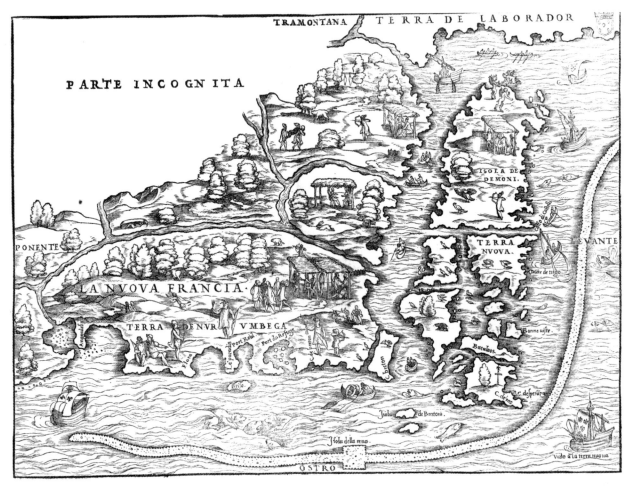

Part of Jacoma di Gastaldi's map of New France, Newfoundland and Labrador, c. 1556. Terra Nuova and the islands to the south of it represent Newfoundland. 'Bonne viste' is named; between 'Bacalos' and 'C. de Speraza' is a Cross or land mark. Centre for Newfoundland Studies, Memorial University of Newfoundland.

islands they were to remain (with certain exceptions) during much of the first century after discovery. He illustrated Indians, birds of prey, and fishing activities but most interesting of all, is a tall cross located north of Cape Race and 'C.de Speranza' but south of 'Bacalaos' and 'Bona Vista', on the east, Atlantic-facing coast. This led E.G.R. Taylor to suggest that Cabot's only landing was at the southern tip of the Avalon Peninsula, with a departure for home from Cape Bauld (Taylor, 1963).

It is unlikely that we will ever know with absolute certainty where Cabot made his landfall, and where he sailed afterwards. The direct evidence is too scanty and, as we have seen, can be used to make a case for a southern landfall, in Cape Breton or further south; for a landfall in the area of the Straits of Belle Isle; and for an eastern landfall, at Cape Bonavista or a point on the Avalon Peninsula. All we can deal with is likelihoods, adding to the documentary evidence modern knowledge of the sea, and of Cabot's navigational methods. Taking everything into consideration, however, we know that Cabot coasted for about a month after his arrival, that he found most of the land on the way back to England,

and that he was rewarded for finding 'the new isle'. This was the great discovery of 1497. It absorbed most of Cabot's attention, and its extent was confirmed by coasting which ended so far to the east, that it made possible an open ocean return to Europe in a very short time. With all this in mind, a northern landfall followed by a coasting voyage which proved the extent of the great island by an anticlockwise near-circumnavigation seems, in the present state of knowledge, to be the most likely solution.

In spite of the alternatives, in Newfoundland the Bonavista tradition is deeply engrained:

Out past the lands to sailors known
With compass good and true,
Still westward, westward on he kept,
Whatever breezes blew;

Till on St. John's Day with the sun
Uprose a headland high;
And 'Bonavista', shouted loud
Brave Cabot to the sky[6].

One who did as much as anybody to remind Newfoundlanders of their Cabot heritage was Judge D.W. Prowse. His *History* (1895) ended by calling up the legend as told on the Peninsula itself: 'On the morning of the 24th June 1897 four hundred years will have rolled away since John Cabot first sighted the green Cape of Bonavista; four centuries will have elapsed since the stem of the *Matthew*'s boat grated on the gravelly shore of Keels, and since King's Cove witnessed the setting up of the Royal Ensign...'. It is now 500 years on and it is ironic, perhaps, that we know more about Jacques Cartier's arrival on the other side of the Bonavista Peninsula in 1534.

Where you think Cabot sighted Newfoundland depends on where you start from: 'Consider the perennial controversy that surrounds John Cabot', wrote Theodore Layng, 'no one in this day and age will think it is a matter of great importance to know exactly his route to Canada or where he landed, but when all the pieces of the puzzle are laid out for inspection, it is a good mental exercise, and good fun, to attempt an answer' (Layng, 1963).

ith following winds, the *Matthew* returned across the Atlantic in 15 days and Cabot went onwards to see the king. When Columbus returned he had been away for just over seven months, and was received at Barcelona in triumph. Cabot had been away only two and a half months and when he caught up with Henry VII it was still high summer. If his Venetian mariner had not brought home profits from great bales of silk or mountains of spices, neither had Columbus, and the king would have been pleased to learn that there were indeed islands in the western ocean which, with timber and fish, could be used as English stepping-stones to even better fortunes.

Henry's daybooks dated August 10-11 read 'Item: to hym that founde the new isle – x li' (£10). Later, he rewarded Cabot with a pension of £20. Cabot pressed the need for a stronger expedition to pursue the great goal of Cathay. Back in Bristol, the impact of the discovery would have been even greater than in London, since the city could expect great prosperity through a new and direct trade with the Far East. The master pilot was regarded as we in our age regarded the first astronauts: '...he is called the Great Admiral and vast honour is paid to him', wrote Pasqualigo to Venice, 'and he goes dressed in silk, and these English run after him like mad...'.

Cabot gained his second letters patent on 3 February, 1498. He was granted powers to 'take at his pleasure vi englisshe shippes in any port or portes... with their apparaill requisite and necessarie for the saveconduct of the seid shippes, and theym convey and lede to the londe and iles of late founde by the seid John...'. The six ships became five and they set sail in May. In July, Pedro de Ayala wrote to the Spanish sovereigns to say that the fleet was provisioned for a

This yere the kyng at the besy request and supplicacion
of a Straunger Venisian which by a caart
made hym self expert in knowyng of the world caused
the kyng to manne a ship wt vytaill & other necessaries
for to seche an Iland wherein the said Straunger
surmysed to be grete comodities / wt which ship
by the kyngs grace so rygged went iii or iiii moo owte
of Bristowe the said Straunger beyng conditor of
the said flete / wherein dyvers merchauntes aswell of
london as Bristowe aventured goodes & sleyght
merchaundises which departed from the west
Cuntrey in the begynnyng of Somer but to thys
present goveth came neuer knoledge of theyr exployt

Passage from a manuscript chronicle reporting that Cabot had not returned. Cotton Mss.

year, but that one 'has made land in Ireland in a great storm with the ship badly damaged. The Genoese kept on his way...it is hoped that they will be back in September'.

It is not known where Cabot's third and last expedition went, or what it achieved. Polydore Vergil (*Anglia Historia*, 1512) wrote that 'he is believed to have found the new lands nowhere but on the very bottom of the ocean', and asserted (contrary to Ayala) that it was Cabot's ship which put back into an Irish port. Williamson (1962) concluded that Cabot did indeed cross the Atlantic to add to his discoveries, which many assume to have been beyond Newfoundland and Cape Breton. News of these discoveries, brought back by survivors of the expedition, would explain, for example, the unnamed, unflagged coast on the La Cosa map.

Other evidence is the return of Gaspar Corte Real's expedition in 1501 with European artifacts obtained from Indians – a piece of a broken gilt sword probably made in Italy, and a pair of silver ear-rings of Venetian manufacture. These could have been obtained in Newfoundland, Labrador or Nova Scotia – though Pietro Pasqualigo, who recorded this news, thought the articles had travelled across Asia. Williamson thought the recovery of these items was possible evidence that one of Cabot's ships had landed in North America in 1498, since there had been no contact with Indians in 1497. But there is always the possibility that men from Bristol had been there before Cabot.

Thin evidence has not prevented a great deal of speculation about the 1498 voyage, which usually links Cabot (the sword), his youngest son, Sancius (the ear-rings), and a landing or shipwreck. The best of these reconstructions is by the geographer Arthur Davies (1955), who connected the voyage to an early 16th century map of the North Atlantic by the Portuguese cartographer Pedro Reinel. This shows 18 place names, some of which Davies argued had Cabot associations, as well as presenting a sequence of saints' days. He suggested that Cabot coasted south along the east coast of Newfoundland, and that his ship went down at sea not far from Grates Cove. The suggestion that Cabot, Sancius and some of the crew got ashore there rests on the authenticity of the Grates Cove rock, still in position in the 1960s, but now missing. It apparently bore inscriptions including 'Io. Cabotto' and other names, including 'Sancius' and 'Sainmalia'. Davies thought the last was the remains of 'Santa Maria save us', or some such expression, a cry for help, and that the party was soon after killed by Indians.

Davies goes on to argue that one of the original fleet wintered in Newfoundland, and then went on to explore the North American coast, reaching latitude 38° N before returning. According to Hakluyt, the ship brought back 'three men taken in the new found Island... These were clothed in beastes skinnes, and ate raw fleshe, and spake such speech that no man coulde understand them, and in their demeanour like to bruit beastes, whom the king kept a time after. Of the which upon two yeeres past after I saw apparelled after the manner of Englishmen, in Westminster pallace, which at that time I could not discern from Englishmen...' (Williamson, 1962).

Davies' account is highly speculative. Nevertheless, it is clear that John Cabot died on the expedition, that further exploration took place, and that the results were reported back. Assuming that 'the voyagers explored the coast west and southwards as they meant to do, we know what they found: primeval tracts and Indian tribes, no great state or government, no cities, seaports, ships or trade, no spices and silks for barter – in a word, no Asia' (Williamson, 1962). Only fish. It was becoming clear that what Cabot had found was not Asia at all, but a new continent. For the English court and the merchants of Bristol, this was a considerable disappointment – though not, some would argue, unexpected (Ryan, 1996). Henry VII became less keen to sponsor voyages of exploration, and Bristol merchants were for the most part interested in trade, not fishing.

he exploration of northeastern America was continued immediately by the Portuguese, who no doubt thought that the new coasts belonged to them under the Treaty of Tordesillas. In 1501 Gaspar Corte Real explored the east coast of Newfoundland and the Labrador coast, perhaps as far north as Hudson Strait (da Mota, 1965). He lost his life, as did his brother Miguel in 1502, his surviving ships returning with new information for the cartographers.

Not all Bristolians lost interest. In 1502 there is the first record of an official, or patent-backed Bristol fishing voyage to Newfoundland by the *Gabriell*. It is probable that there were more ships as well in later years, but because they had no license to fish at Newfoundland, they were listed at the Bristol custom house as coming from Ireland (Ruddock, 1974). Together with some Azorians, Bristol merchants also set up a 'Company of Adventurers into the New Found Islands'.

Sebastian Cabot (c 1482-1557), who may or may not have sailed with his father in 1497 and 1498, remained in England until 1510, when he went to Spain. He served Henry VII as a cartographer, and in 1505 received an annuity for service to the Crown 'in and about the fyndinge of the newe founde landes to our full good pleasure'. This indicates either his involvement in a voyage to Newfoundland before April 1505 with the company (Ruddock, in Quinn 1993), or that he had prepared maps of the Bristol voyages which indicated that a new continent had been found, or perhaps both.

The Company of Adventurers did not survive, and the English fishery at Newfoundland developed slowly during the 16th century. The importation of cod to Portugal by 1506 was, however, sufficient to warrant the imposition of a new fish tax. Meanwhile, fishermen from Portugal, Spain, France and England shared many small harbours in Newfoundland, with the English using the southernmost, Atlantic-facing shores. The

French were prominent in this area too, as well as at St. John's and to the west and south of the Avalon Peninsula, where they shared harbours with the Basques, whose cod fishery had begun by the 1520s. As the century progressed, they established whaling stations in western Newfoundland and in south Labrador.

Maritime explorers continued to search north and west. In 1508, Sebastian Cabot attempted the North-west Passage and may have entered Hudson Bay. His crew refused to go further, and he then coasted south at least as far as Cape Hatteras, clearly looking for another passage to Asia. He was the first to sail back to England by way of the Gulf Stream. Other Englishmen eventually followed this lead, including Frobisher (1576-1578) and Davis (1567-1585).

During the 1530s the French began seriously to explore the region, rather than looking for ways around it, their efforts leading eventually to the colonisation of Acadia and New France. Sir Humphrey Gilbert officially staked – perhaps re-staked – the English claim to Newfoundland in 1583 on behalf of Queen Elizabeth I.

In Bristol, interest in Newfoundland revived in the late 16th century. Among charitable enterprises urged there in 1595 was the recruitment of a clergyman to minister to the sailors about to set off for Newfoundland (Vanes, 1977). Soon after, the merchants backed the London and Bristol Company of Adventurers to Newfoundland, which sent out John Guy to govern their settlement at Cuper's Cove (Cupids). The opportunities of the Atlantic had become an 'ever-widening gate' (Sacks, 1993). Ultimately, Bristolians, like other Englishmen, owed a significant debt to the Genoese John Cabot.

Over the same period, the geographic realities of the region unfolded and became accepted. The Portuguese at first called Newfoundland and Labrador 'Terra Corte Real', and called Greenland 'Labrador' until the 1570s. The Cantino world-chart of 1502 is the earliest Portuguese map to show Newfoundland as an island ('Terra del Rey de portuguall') covered with trees and free-standing in mid-Atlantic, beyond which in a lower latitude are Columbus' islands, leading towards a projection of Asia. But in the south is Brazil, decorated with the parrots and trees reported by Cabral, the Portuguese navigator who found it in 1500 when blown off course. It is ironic but true, that if Columbus had not found his 'Indies' the Portuguese would have discovered the North American mainland by following the coasts to the north.

As for the name 'Newfoundland', it seems to have evolved from Cabot's 'new isle' of 1497. His 1498 letters patent used 'land' in the phrase 'the londe and isles of late founde by the said John' – 'londe' meaning mainland or island, as in 1502, when a grant used four separate words: 'the newe found launde'. There is no doubt thereafter of fish being brought from the 'Newfounde lleond'. The form 'Terra Nova' was attached by the Portuguese by 1506, 'Tierra Neuva' by the Spaniards in 1511 at the latest, and 'Terre-Neufsve' by the French in 1510 (Story, 1982).

In 1506, the printed world map by Contarini still showed the new lands north of the Spanish discoveries as part of the eastern horn of Asia, but the huge bulk of South America had emerged clearly as a new southern continent. It was Martin Waldseemuller, cosmographer at the University of St. Die (in the Vosges), who broke from precedent to install two new continents between Europe and Asia, calling the southern one 'America' on his world map of 1507. The name would soon be applied to both new continents and it came from a Florentine in Seville, Amerigo Vespucci, who sailed to South America with Hojeda (who himself had sailed with Columbus). Vespucci wrote an egotistical account of his voyage, pre-dated it, and circulated it in Europe (Smithsonian, 1983). In it he claimed to have 'found a continent' which 'we may rightly call a new world'. Waldseemuller saw 'no reason why we should not call this other part...America after the sagacious discoverer Americus'. Though Vespucci had called himself Albericus Vespucius in his earlier writings, the new name took hold: and a continent whose natives were misnamed 'Indians' acquired not the name of Columbus or Cabot, its actual discoverers, but that of a pretender.

But there are other versions. The name has also been said to derive from a Nicaraguan word meaning 'land rich in gold', or from the name of one of the

Indian tribes encountered by the earliest explorers. Still another brings us back to Cabot. When the 400th anniversary of Cabot's discovery was being celebrated, an ancient manuscript was found at Westminster Abbey. It was the customs rolls of the port of Bristol for 1496 to 1499, recording two payments of £20 to John Cabot on behalf of King Henry VII from the Collectors of Customs (Hudd, 1909). The senior official who actually handed over the money to the discoverer was Richard Ameryk.

The entry in Henry VII's Daybook granting Cabot £10..

n 1893, the Rev. Dr. Moses Harvey, the Newfoundland writer, read a paper before the Historical Society of Nova Scotia urging that a Cabot celebration be held in 1897:

Surely the northern people will not permit the year 1897 to pass without some worthy celebration in grateful recollection of the man who first opened Northern America to European civilization. It would be no more than an act of tardy justice; for it is discreditable to England that one of the bravest of her sailors, who gave her a continent, has never yet had the smallest honour conferred upon his name, or the most insignificant recognition of the vast services he rendered to his adopted country...Not a cape, headland, gulf, or creek in the wide region to which they led the way bears the name of Cabot, with the exception of a small, rocky islet off the eastern coast of Newfoundland, to which the name Cabot Island was recently given. No statue or monument has been raised to the memory of either father or son (Harvey, 1895).

Harvey repeated this message to the Royal Society of Canada, which was to meet in Halifax in the summer of 1897. When he was joined by Sir Sandford Fleming and others, the bandwagon began to roll. 'How should we celebrate?' inevitably became mixed up with 'Where did Cabot make his landfall?', and the divergence of opinion on the second question made it difficult to agree on the first. The debate spread through the Atlantic region's newspapers, and as far as Toronto and Montreal (Perin, 1990).

In Newfoundland during the fall of 1896, the discussion pitted the Roman Catholic bishop, M.F.

Howley (for Cape St. John), against Harvey (for Cape Breton); and Harvey, who thought Sebastian Cabot's evidence could be trusted, disputed with the historian Judge D.W. Prowse, who supported a Bonavista landfall and was dubious about Sebastian Cabot's veracity. Both Howley and Prowse attacked the Canadians Dawson and Harrisse. Harvey protested that he and Prowse remained fast friends, but some thought the exchanges too precious, one reader accusing Prowse of puffing up his recently published *History of Newfoundland.* A fair point, since, in his next letter, Prowse commented that a reviewer in England favoured a big celebration in the colony. The St. John's balladeer, Johnny Burke, refused to take the dispute seriously:

There's an argument unfinished
'Twixt his lordship and the judge,
And the doctor takes a hand in
For to settle an old grudge.
It's about this Cabot landfall
They are making such a racket;
Some say he came as passenger
In Billy Coady's packet.

At the Mechanics' Hall, a billiard match settled the issue in favour of Bonavista.

There was uncertainty over the form of a permanent memorial for the event. The Fishermen's Society at Bonavista installed a plaque in their hall reading '1497 – Landfall of Cabot – 1897', and there was talk of erecting a much-vaunted breakwater and light there. Harvey refused to support this, knowing that an obelisk was being considered for Sydney, Nova Scotia, and campaigned for a similar structure on Signal Hill in St. John's – 'one of the noblest sites for such a memorial, overlooking our beautiful harbour, and commanding a view that is unsurpassed in the great Atlantic...'. But the obelisk faded before a 'day and night signal station', soon to be called the 'Cabot Memorial Observation and Signal Station' and finally the 'Cabot Signal Tower and Meteorological Observatory'.

In the meantime, the Newfoundland Cabot Committee had been upstaged. The Royal Society of Canada invited representatives from Bristol and British historical and geographical societies, as well as officials from the

United States, all Canadian provinces and Newfoundland, to celebrations at Halifax, where a commemorative brass plate was to be placed in the Provincial Building. In Toronto there was to be a Cabot exhibition, while in Bristol there were to be Cabot celebrations and a memorial, with a £50 prize for the best suggestions.

As a prime mover in Newfoundland, Prowse faced some opposition, so it was a comfort to find out that in Bristol 'The difficulties they have had to encounter are ludicrously like our own – rival projects, carping critics and a general endeavour to throttle and stifle the project'. There was a late run of support for a 'St. John's Cabot Market', and one wag suggested a great watergate for the Narrows 'to keep the cold air out of St. John's'. What eventually emerged in Bristol and St. John's were Cabot towers, each of which still draws thousands of visitors annually.

It was a problem everywhere that the Cabot centenary coincided with Queen Victoria's Diamond Jubilee. Both were celebrated on Brandon Hill in Bristol, where the foundation stone of an imposing tower was laid by the Marquis of Dufferin and Ava on 24 June in the presence of 50,000 people. Premier Sir William Whiteway of Newfoundland, along with other leaders of the Empire, was invited to participate in the Jubilee ceremonies in London, and missed the ceremonies in St. John's. Governor Sir Hubert Murray decided that he could only attend the dedication of the Victoria wing at the General Hospital, which was the official Jubilee project, and ungenerously refused an invitation to climb Signal Hill on 22 June to help lay the tower's foundation stone.

Others were more enthusiastic. A united city choir was present, and several reprises of the national anthem were led by the 'Twillingate Nightingale', Georgina Stirling. The music interspersed some long speeches by Edgar Bowring, Judge Prowse, Bishop Howley and Moses Harvey (read for him).

All the speeches were liberally sprayed with Cabotan mythology designed to confirm and foster the legitimacy of the Anglo-Saxon supremacy in the New World begun by (the Italian) Cabot at Newfoundland, the 'Cornerstone of Empire'. Indeed, the 'myth was translated into ritual and commemorated in stone' (Smrz, 1994). Both in St. John's and Halifax, speakers dwelled on the virtues of the race and of an Empire upon which the sun never set (Williams, 1996). Prowse had already reflected the same sentiments in his *History*. Cabot's voyage, he wrote, 'gave North America to the English by right of discovery. How different might have been the future of this great continent...had Columbus ...discovered it?'. Newfoundland could have ended up a 'great Spanish possession, with chronic revolutions, disordered finances, pronunciamentos, half-breeds and fusillades' (Prowse, 1895).

As for the rest of the joint celebrations, there were parades by the Constabulary and the fire brigade, loyal addresses at Government House, and the Royal Navy fired torpedoes from pinnaces attached to HMS *Cordelia* and HMS *Buzzard*. The public buildings were lit up in the evening and bonfires crowned the adjoining hills. For people in the principal outports there were fireworks; and for the upper crust there was a Jubilee ball attended by the officers of the British, French and American vessels in port.

In Halifax, the ceremonies fell behind schedule. The army and navy paraded in honour of the Governor-General and a galaxy of distinguished guests. In the afternoon, Archbishop O'Brien gave his Presidential Address to the Royal Society and university representatives from the USA and Canada. Unfortunately, the Governor-General consistently spoke of 'Cabo', as if he were French, and of Sebastian as if he were John's brother, after which the Bristol delegates (Messrs Barker and Davies) took a long time to assert their claim on the Cabots as true Bristolians. 'If Cabot had been in Halifax today', wrote an American correspondent, 'he'd have been talked to death'.

here have been more recent commemorative plaques located in Nova Scotia, Newfoundland and Québec (linked with the Italo-Canadian community), and the story of the Cabots has attracted verse, painting, statuary and street-names. Community reminders, unavoidable for years in Bristol and in Canada, are also present in London where one of Europe's biggest commercial developments (Canary Wharf) is grouped around Cabot Square. In Atlantic Canada, the most conspicuous reminders of the widespread claim on Cabot are the Cabot Highway – or 'Discovery Trail' – which beckons the tourist to Bonavista, and the Cabot Trail which winds its way through the Cape Breton Highlands National Park.

The 1897 Newfoundland postage stamps have become collectors' items, not least because the two cent, labelled 'Cabot – Hym That Found The New Isle',

1897 commemorative stamp with a portrait of (Sebastian) Cabot.
Thomas F. Nemec, Secretary, St. John's Philatelic Society.

is actually a portrait of Sebastian Cabot. The ten cent stamp – 'Cabot's Ship the *Matthew* Leaving the Avon' – is thought to have been drawn with one of Columbus's ships as the model. In 1947 the five cent Newfoundland commemorative showed Cabot on deck 'Off Cape Bonavista', and in confederation year the *Matthew* reappeared, ploughing the waves on the Canada four cent.

Cabot's departure from Bristol has attracted artists, most notably Ernest Board, whose famous Edwardian painting hangs in Bristol City Museum, and appeared as a frontispiece in the first volume of J.R. Smallwood's *Book of Newfoundland* (1937). Harold Goodridge's 1947 painting of the departure (cover) has recently been re-discovered. A fresh approach for 1997 is Donald McCleod's portrayal of the *Matthew* the night before leaving (page 20).

We do not know what John Cabot looked like. An imaginary medallion portrait by Carlo Pezzi was published in Venice in 1881 (see Sharp, 1991). In the 1970s he was set in bronze outside Confederation Building, St. John's, and at Bonavista, a standing figure gazing out to sea. By contrast, at Bristol he sits pensively, looking westwards, a casual part of the street furniture within touch of the ships tied up at the Quay.

If no genuine portraits of John Cabot have survived, there is a tale about his son. A man who 'lived a fantasy life of mysteries and dark secrets alongside his more prosaic every day activities' (Quinn, 1993) would appreciate what happened to his likeness. Sebastian was painted, presumably from life, wearing the chain of office of the Governor of the Merchant Venturers of London. First hung in Whitehall, the portrait found its way to the home of the Earl of Errol in Scotland before being sold to Charles Joseph Harford of Bristol. Many thought it was by Holbein, and because he believed Sebastian was the discoverer (Biddle, 1831), Richard Biddle of Pittsburg, a Cabot scholar, bought it, and took it to the United States where it was destroyed by fire in 1845.

However, an engraving had appeared in Sayer's *Memoirs of Bristol* (1824), which was reprinted by Nicholls in his Sebastian Cabot memoir (1869), and by Harvey in *Newfoundland – The Oldest British Colony*

(1883). This was the basis for the Newfoundland 1897 postage stamp of 1897. For 400 years and more, the son stood in for his father.

Although Sebastian is the subject of a novel (Smith, 1985), his father has fared better in verse. But if the versifier possessed a way with words and knowledge of what really happened, he or she has also needed hand on the tiller to keep the wind in the sails. Examples are legion from both sides of the Atlantic. In the 1950s, A.C. Wornell earnestly recorded Cabot's 'telepathic thought' at departure, endowing the old mariner with a command of English he would scarcely have possessed. Cabot speaks:

'But now the tide is almost at its height;
The night is fair, the wind is favourable;
The ship is filled with necessary victuals;
The clerk upon the quay has his report;
Our kindred have bestowed their tears and blessings
And we are left alone with Destiny...

'...Thus our resolution merits honour.
Our great determination is to seek
New lands beyond the Western Ocean's rim.
So shall we follow each day's new horizon
Until we furl our sails in NEW FOUND LAND.' [7]

This Cabot was ready to face his fate, and he knew where he was going. There is a more sombre mood in 'North-West Passage', a 63 verse epic written by the prolific novelist, essayist and poet Francis Brett Young (1944), most of whose tales were set in the West Midland counties of England. It is spoken throughout by a member of Cabot's Bristol crew, and is full of halyards screaming, shredded spray and drifting ice, with 'the drunken lodestar full ahead'. The sea subsides, the fog lifts and an unknown shore appears:

So we broached a keg of Gascony
To drink John Cabote's health,
Who had brought us safe through the icy seas
To lands of untold wealth

Where our eyes, he told, might soon behold
Those fabled Cities of Cathay
Where common streets were paved with gold
And flowers bloomed alway...

We know what must come next, but how could a common sailor know, or care, that down the centuries to come, fish would be worth more to his masters and betters than the gold which would soon be wrested from the Indians on the Spanish Main?

For naught was there but a wilderness
Of barren rock, and trackless wood
Where no sound broke the silences
Of a deathlike solitude

But the boom of rollers on the beach
And the scream of seabirds overhead;
That awful silence muted speech
And crushed our hearts with dread.

And yet, home again, with the elder blooming on Clifton Down, our frustrated sailor seems ready, like

Cabot, for another attempt at the lottery of discovery. He can smell the mould of the forest sod afar off and he finds it strangely sweet:

And my nights are lit by the wild gleam
Of the passion that beguiles
The hearts of islanders to dream
Of undiscovered isles

And in those dreams I grope my way
North-westward through the grinding ice
To the Seven Cities of Cathay
And the fabled Isles of Spice.

And then, of course, Cabot's end. In mind or body or spirit was he close to the gravelly shores where the caplin spawn, the driftwood is strewn and the seabirds call?

All honour to this grand old Pilot,
Whose flag is struck, whose sails are furled,
Whose ship is beached, whose voyage ended
Who sleeps somewhere in sod unknown
Without a slab, without a stone,
In that great Island, sea impearled...[8]

There has been a great shift in attitude since the Cabot celebrations of 1897 and 1947. The European arrival in the Americas is no longer seen as a romantic and morally uncomplicated adventure, and the former heroes of the Age of Discovery are the subject of a sometimes hostile analysis primarily concerned with the ambivalent consequences of their achievements, rather than with their actual accomplishments. In this context, Cabot is no longer celebrated as the heroic founder of a great empire, but as the harbinger of a fateful collision between two cultures, the European and the aboriginal, which has had a profound impact upon each. Reflecting the moral uncertainties which now surround the Cabot voyages, as well as the more general values of the 1990s, the 1997 celebrations planned for each side of the Atlantic have relatively little to do with history, and a great deal to do with commercialism. The 'grand old Pilot', once the 'Cornerstone of Empire', has been translated into a neutral tourist opportunity. Is it surprising that no poetry has yet appeared?

Notes:

1 Unsalted, dried codfish.

2 The replica of The *Matthew* built for the 1997 celebrations at Redcliffe Quay, Bristol, is a 75 foot, three-masted vessel. The keel is made of African opepe wood, the frame is oak, and the planking Douglas pine. With only ship models to follow, the designer opted for appearance and performance first, coupled with a closely authentic style of construction.

3 Deviation from true north.

4 A rhumb was about 11 degrees.

5 Except the controversial Vinland map.

6 'Isabel', (St. John's) *Evening Herald*, 20 June, 1897.

7 A.C. Wornell, 'John Cabot, May 2, 1497', in *The Book of Newfoundland* IV (1967).

8 Wilfred Campbell, 'Cabot', 1925.

BIBLIOGRAPHY

Almagia, Roberto. *Commemorazione de Sebastiano Caboto nel IV Centenario Della Morte.* Venice 1958.

Ballesteros-Gaibrois, M. 'Juan Caboto en Espana'. *Revista de Indias* IV, 1943.

Biddle, Richard. *A Memoir of Sebastian Cabot.* London 1831.

Biggar, H.P. *The Precursors of Jacques Cartier, 1497-1534.* Ottawa 1911.

Boorstin, Daniel J. *The Discoverers.* New York 1983.

Burpee, L.J. 'John Cabot, who sought Cipangu, and found Canada'. *Canadian Geographical Journal* 5, 1933.

Carus-Wilson, E.M. *The Merchant Adventurers of Bristol in the Fifteenth Century.* Bristol 1962.

Cortesao, A. 'The pre-Columbian discovery of America'. *Geographical Journal* 88, 1937.

Crone, G.R. 'The Vinland Map Cartographically Considered'. *Geographical Journal* 132, 1966.

Cumming, W.P., Skelton,R.A. and Quinn, D.B. *The Discovery of North America.* Toronto and Montreal 1971.

Da Mota, A. Teixeira. 'Portuguese Navigations in the North Atlantic in the Fifteenth and Sixteenth Centuries'. Lecture given at Memorial University. St. John's 1965.

Davies, Arthur. 'The Last Voyage of John Cabot and the Rock at Grates Cove'. *Nature* CLXXVI, 1955.

Davies, Arthur. 'The Vinland Map and the Tartar Relation: a review'. *Geography* 51, 1966.

Dawson, S.E. *The Voyages of the Cabots: Latest Phases of the Controversy.* Ottawa, Toronto, London 1897.

English, L.E.F. 'The Land First Seen'. *Newfoundland Stories and Ballads.* St. John's 1962.

Forbes Taylor, F.R. 'Bristol fishermen on the Grand Banks'. (London) *Times,* 15 April, 1976.

Gallo, Rodolfo. 'Intorno a Giovanni Caboto'. *Rendiconti Accad. Naz. dei Lincei, Cl.di Sc.Morali* III, 1948.

Ganong, W.F. *Crucial Maps in the Early Cartography and Place-Nomenclature of the Atlantic Coast of Canada.* Toronto 1964.

Harrisse, Henry. *Découverte et évolution cartographique de Terre-Neuve et des pays circonvoisins, 1497-1769.* Paris 1890.

Harrisse, Henry. *The Discovery of North America....* London 1892.

Harrisse, Henry. *John Cabot, the Discoverer of North America and Sebastian his Son.* London 1896.

Harris, Leslie. 'The Cabot Landfall: an Examination of the Evidence'. Lecture to Newfoundland Historical Society, 1967.

Harris, R. Cole. *Historical Atlas of Canada I. From the Beginning to 1800.* Toronto 1987.

Harvey, Rev. M. 'The Voyages and Discoveries of the Cabots'. *Collections of the Nova Scotia Historical Society* IX, 1895.

Howley, M.F. 'Latest lights on the Cabot Controversy'.

Transactions of the Royal Society of Canada. Second series, 9, 1903.

Hudd, A.E. 'Richard Ameryk and the name America'. *Proceedings of the Clifton Antiquarian Club* 7:1, 1909-10.

Ingstad, Helge. *Westward to Vinland.* London 1969.

Jackson, Melvin H. 'The Labrador Landfall of John Cabot: the 1497 Voyage Reconsidered'. *Canadian Historical Review* XLIV: 2, 1963.

Jones, Gwyn. *The Norse Atlantic Saga.* Toronto 1964.

Larsen, Sofus. *The Discovery of America Twenty Years Before Columbus.* Copenhagen and London 1925.

Layng, Theodore E. 'Charting the course [of John Cabot] to Canada'. *Congresso Internacional de Historia dos Descobrimentos II Actas,* 1965

Little, Bryan. *John Cabot: the Reality.* Bristol 1983.

Markham, Clements R.(ed.). *The Journals of Christopher Columbus.* Hakluyt Society, London 1893.

McGhee, R. and Tuck, J. 'Did the Medieval Irish Visit Newfoundland ?'. *Canadian Geographic,* June-July 1977.

McGrath, Patrick. 'Bristol and America, 1480-1631'. In Andrews, K.R. et al.(eds.). *The Westward Enterprise: English Activities in Ireland, the Atlantic, and America, 1480-1650.* Liverpool 1978.

McManis, Douglas R. 'The Traditions of Vinland'. *Geographical Review* 59: 4, 1969.

Melgaard, Jorgen. *Fra Brattahild til Vinland.* Copenhagen 1961.

Morison, Samuel Eliot. *Portuguese Voyages to America in the Fifteenth Century.* Cambridge, Mass. 1940.

Morison, Samuel Eliot. *Admiral of the Ocean Sea: A Life of Christopher Columbus.* Boston 1942.

Morison, Samuel Eliot. *The European Discovery of America: The Northern Voyages, 500-1600 AD.* New York 1971.

Munn, W.A. 'John Cabot's landfall'. Lecture to Newfoundland Historical Society. *Newfoundland Quarterly* 36:1, 1936.

Nicholls, J.F. *The Remarkable Life, Adventures and Discoveries of Sebastian Cabot.* Bristol 1869.

Nunn, George E. *The Mappemonde of Juan de la Cosa.* Jenkintown 1943.

O'Dea, Fabian. 'Cabot's Landfall – Yet Again'. In Barbara Farrell and Aileen Desbarats (eds.). *Explorations in the History of Canadian Mapping: A Collection of Essays.* Ottawa 1988.

Perin, Roberto. 'La decouverte Canadienne de Jean Cabot ou les emplois de l'histoire'. *Atti del Convegno Venezia El Caboto. Le Relazioni Italo-Canadesi.* Venice 1990

Prowse, D.W. *A History of Newfoundland from the English, Colonial and Foreign Records.* London 1895.

Quinn, D.B. 'The Croft voyage of 1481'. *The Mariner's Mirror,* XXI, 1935.

Quinn, D.B. 'The argument for the English discovery of America between 1480 and 1494'. *Geographical Journal* CXXVII: 3, 1961.

Quinn, D.B. *North America from Earliest Discovery to First Settlements.* New York 1977.

Quinn, D.B. *Sebastian Cabot and Bristol Exploration.* Revised edition. Bristol 1993.

Ruddock, Alwyn A. 'John Day of Bristol and the English Voyages across the Atlantic before 1497'. *Geographical Journal* CXXXII, 1966.

Ruddock, Alwyn A. 'The Reputation of Sebastian Cabot'. *Bulletin of the Institute of Historical Research* 47, 1974.

Ryan, A.N. 'Bristol, the Atlantic and North America, 1480-1509'. In J.B. Hattendorf (ed.). *Maritime History I: The Age of Discovery.* Malabar, Florida. 1996.

Sacks, Davis Harris. *The Widening Gate: Bristol and the Atlantic Economy, 1450-1700.* Los Angeles 1993.

Severin, Tim. *The Brendan Voyage.* London 1978.

Sharp, J.J. *Discovery in the North Atlantic.* Halifax, N.S. 1991.

Skelton, R.A., Marston T.E. and Painter, G.D. *The Vinland Map and the Tartar Relation.* New Haven and London 1995 (new edition).

Skelton, R.A. 'John Cabot'. *Dictionary of Canadian Biography* I, 1966.

Smith, A.C.H. *Sebastian the Navigator.* London 1985.

Smithsonian Institution. *The Naming of America.* 1983.

Smrz, Jiri. 'Cabot and Newfoundland Identity: The 1897 Celebrations'. BA dissertation, Memorial University 1994.

Story, G.M.(ed.). *Early European Settlement and Exploration in Atlantic Canada: Selected Papers.* Memorial University, St. John's 1982.

Taylor, E.G.R. 'Where did the Cabots go? A Study in Historical Deduction'. *Geographical Journal* 129, 1963.

Taylor, E.G.R. 'The Vinland Map'. *Journal of the Institute of Navigation* 27:2, 1974.

Toque, Rev. P. *Newfoundland, as it was and as it is in 1877.* Toronto 1878.

Vanes, Jean. *The Port of Bristol in the Sixteenth Century.* Bristol 1977.

Vigneras, Louis-Andre. 'New Light on the 1497 Cabot Voyage to America'. *Hispanic-American Historical Review* XXXVI: 4, 1956.

Vigneras, Louis-Andre. 'The Cape Breton Landfall: 1494 or 1497? Note on a Letter by John Day'. *Canadian Historical Review* XXXVIII: 3, 1957.

Williams, A.F. 'Cabot 500: Myths, Traditions and Celebrations'. Canada House lecture, London 1996.

Williamson, J.A. 'John Cabot, the Discoverer of North America'. In Williamson. *Builders of the British Empire.* London 1925.

Williamson, J.A. *The Voyages of the Cabots and the English Discovery of North America under Henry VII and Henry VIII.* Cambridge 1929.

Williamson, J.A. *The Cabot Voyages and Bristol Discovery under Henry VII.* Hakluyt Society, Cambridge 1962.

Young, Francis Brett. *The Island.* London 1944.